Jumpe

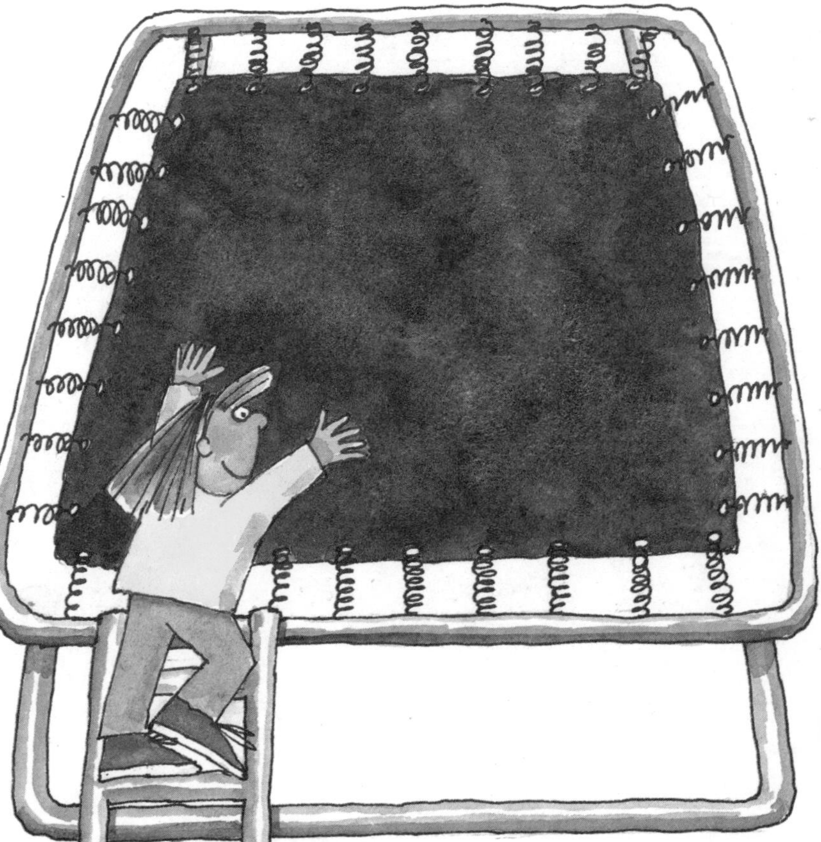

By Karen Anderson

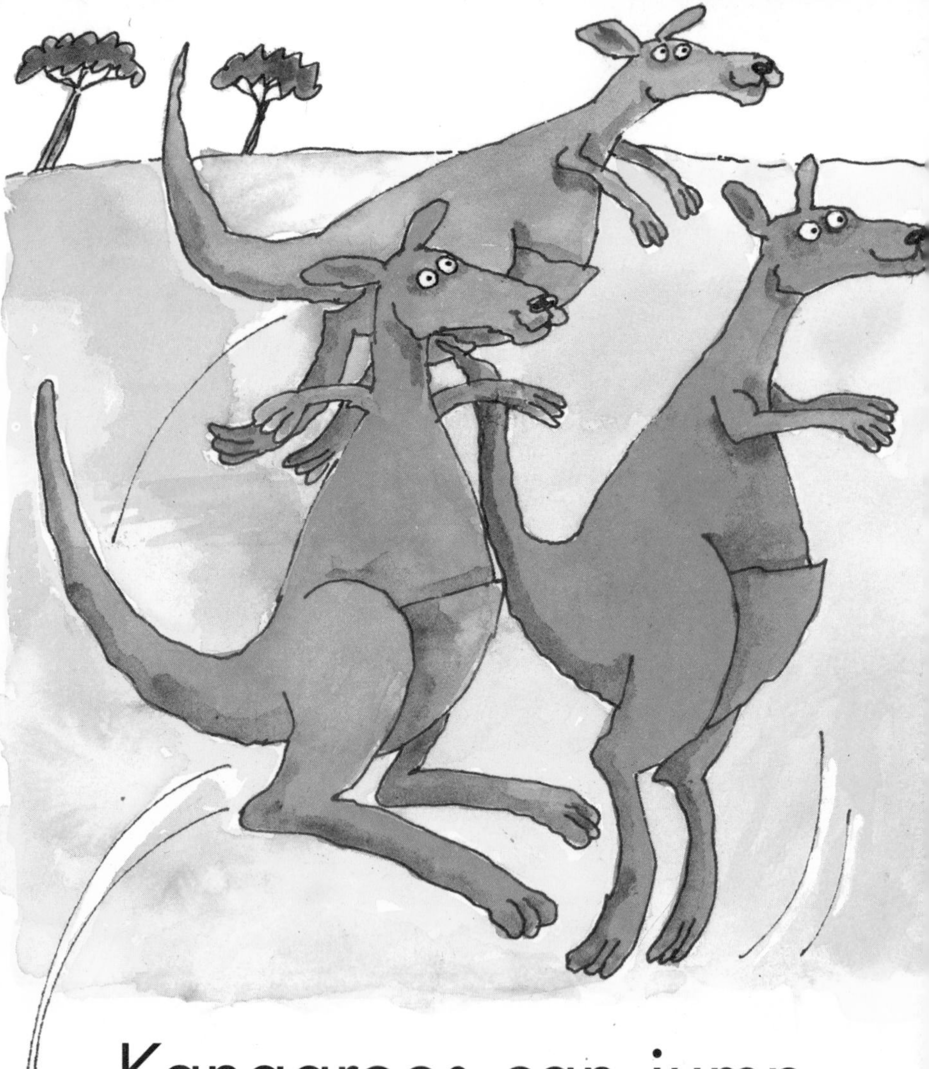

Kangaroos can jump.

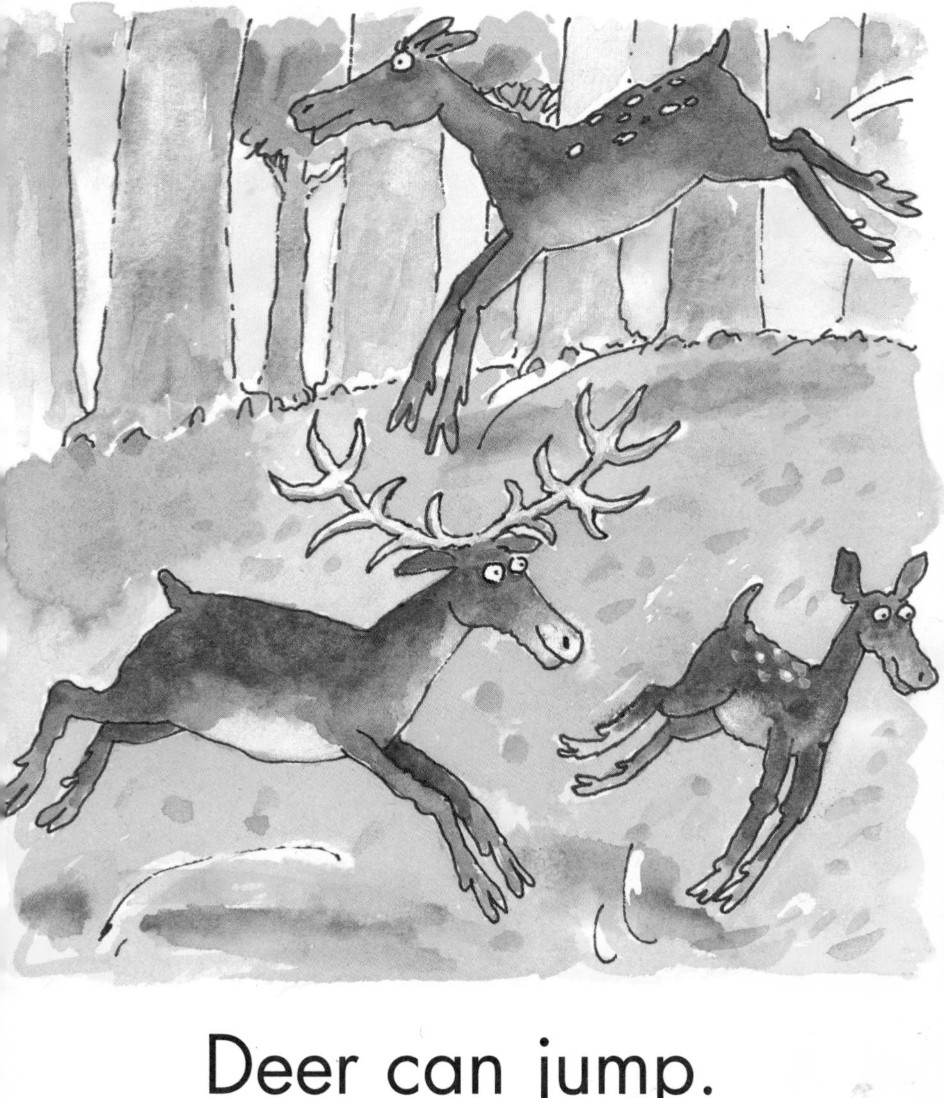

Deer can jump.

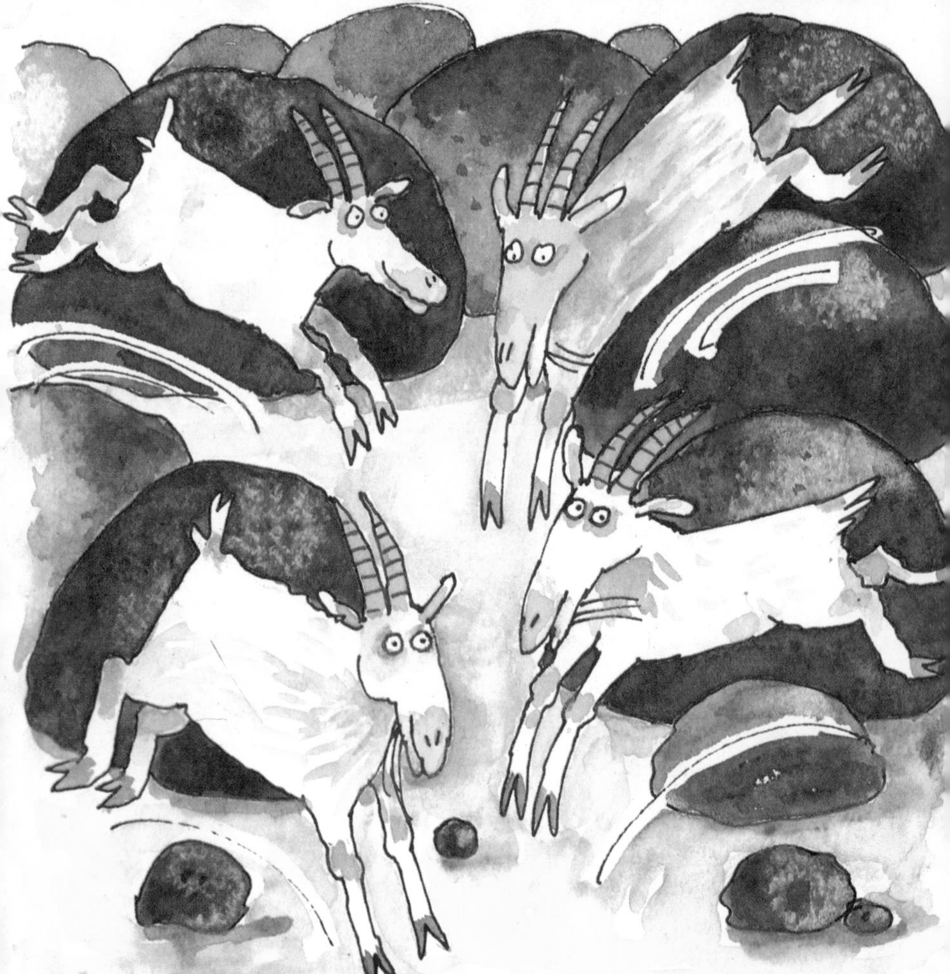

Goats can jump.

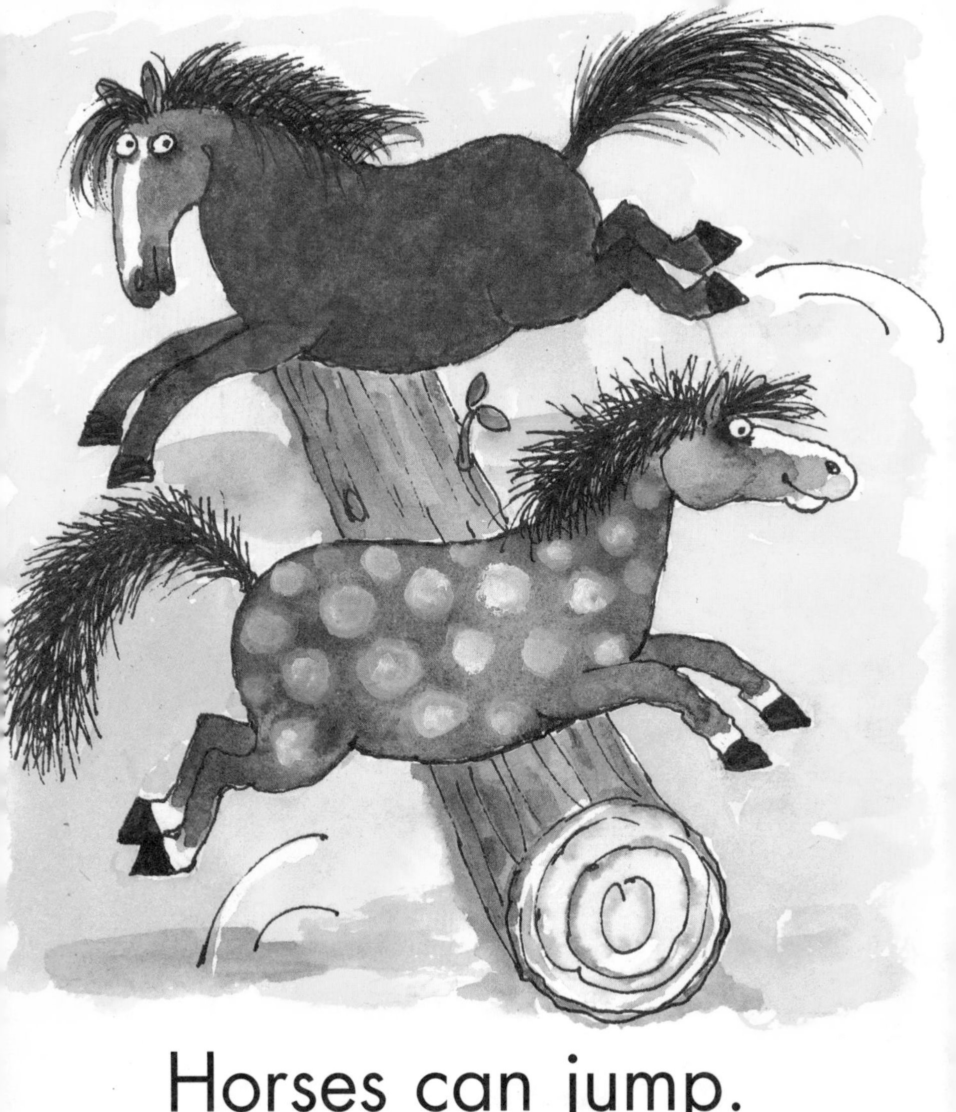

Horses can jump.

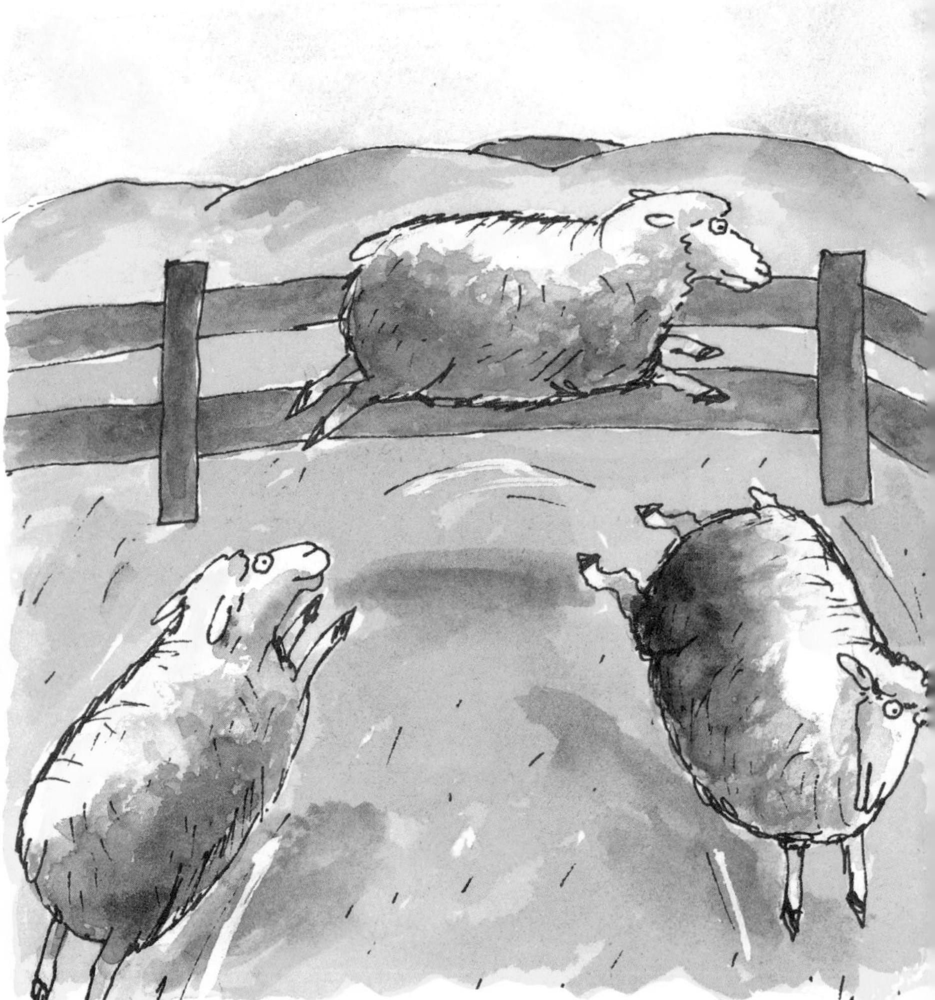

Sheep can jump.

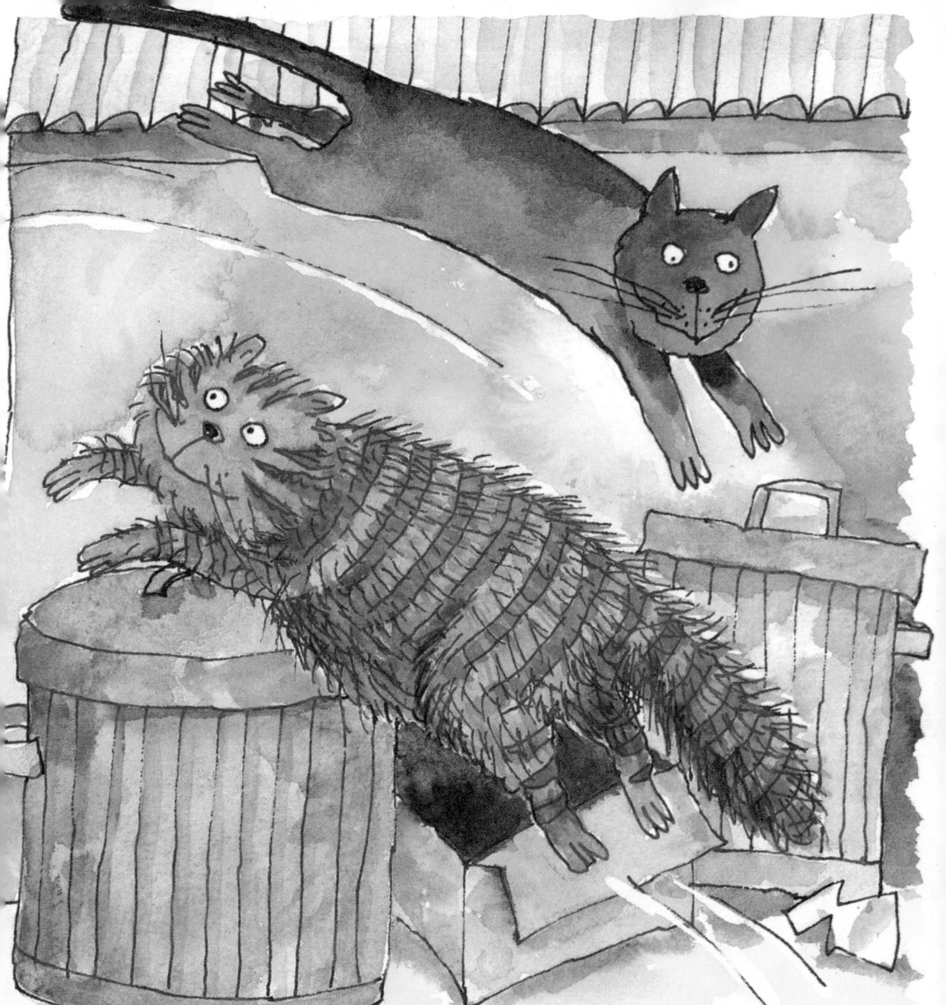

Cats can jump.

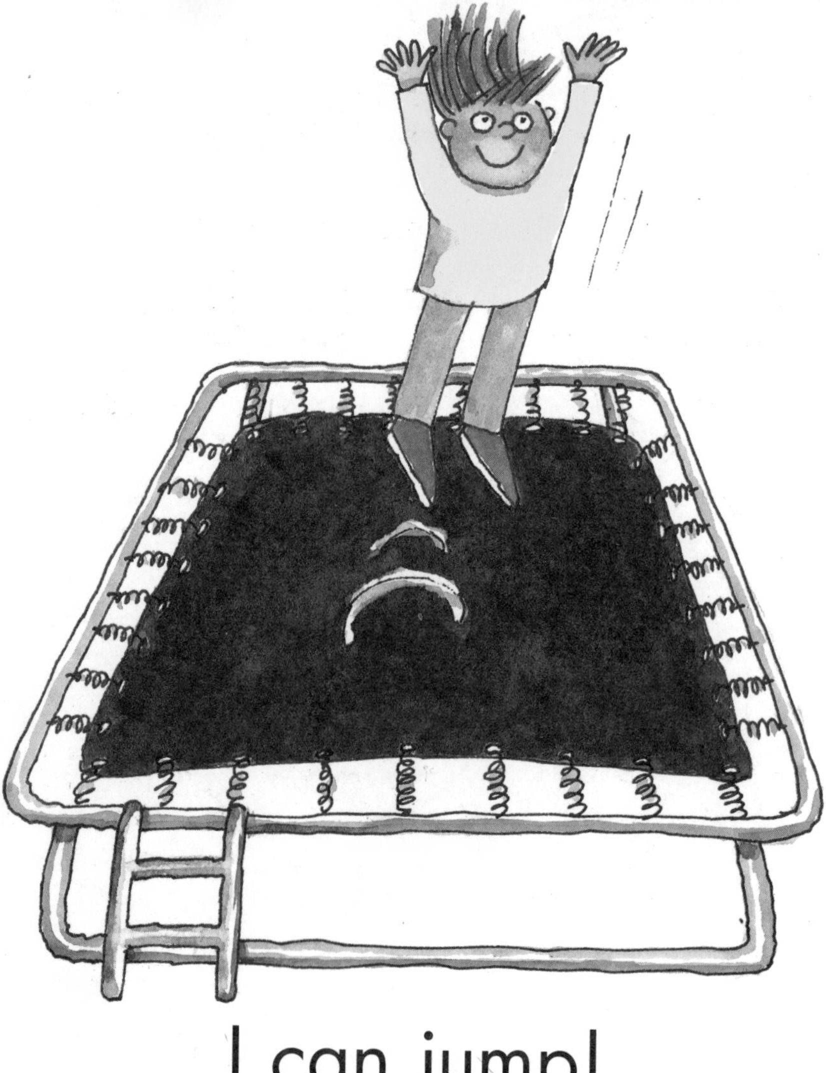

I can jump!